Science Technology Engineering Math
STEM STARTERS FOR KIDS

TECHNOLOGY
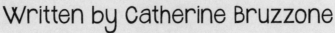
ACTIVITY
Book

Written by Catherine Bruzzone

Designed and illustrated by
Vicky Barker

R
FOR
YOUNG
READERS

ISBN
978-1-63158-682-8

WHAT IS TECHNOLOGY?

Technology is the practical application of scientific knowledge by engineers and scientists. Their aim is to improve the things around us. Touchscreen mobile phones are a good example of how technology can make our lives easier. Or the simple and humble door hinge!

Not all technology is shiny and digital. The best inventions are those that everybody can benefit from. There is a lot of technology that is very impressive but that not everybody can afford to use like fancy cars or sophisticated sound systems for listening to music. One other thing to think about is that technology is not always the product that we are using. A lot of industries rely on new technology in order to provide us with new and exciting products. It might not be obvious at first but hi-tech machines are necessary to create things like coloring pencils, chargers or even our favorite sweets.

WHAT IS STEM?

STEM stands for "science, technology, engineering and mathematics." These four areas are closely linked: new discoveries in science give technology and engineering new things to invent to make our lives easier and the world a better place. However, you could say that mathematics is the most important one as no scientist or engineer could do their job properly without it!

Science

Technology

Engineering

Math

UNDER PRESSURE

We use taps to turn the water on and off in our homes. The taps are attached to the hot and cold water pipes. Inside each tap are two discs with holes in them. When you turn the tap, the discs slide across each other to open or close the holes. The water in the pipes is under pressure. This means it is pushing against the discs in the tap. So when the discs line up and the hole opens, it gushes out.

Follow this safe drinking water on its journey from tap to plughole.

TOILET TROUBLES

The modern toilet means we can flush away our wastewater (poo and pee) safely and keep our neighborhoods clean and free from disease. In the past, wastewater would be thrown into the streets and it was impossible to stop horrible smells. Now when you flush the toilet, the water rushes into the bowl and clears out the wastewater. This runs along pipes out of the house, under the street and to a special sewage treatment center. This treats the water until it's clean enough to go back into the rivers again.

Toilets are very important! Do you know enough about them to answer these questions?

(Answers on page 30.)

1. When is World Toilet Day?

a) 9th August

b) 19th November

c) 1st April

d) 17th October

2. On average, how many years of your life do you spend on the toilet?

a) half a year

b) three years

c) five years

d) twelve years

5. What else does the technology used to make toilet brushes also make?

a) artificial trees

b) toothbrushes

c) rulers

d) plastic jewellery

3. What did the Vikings use instead of toilet paper (which hadn't been invented yet)?

a) a wide stick

b) big leaves

c) sheep's wool

d) animal skins

4. Which of these things carries more germs than an average toilet seat?

a) mobile phone

b) computer keyboard

c) washing up sponge

d) pet food bowl

5

CATCH!

Medieval castles and cities were defended by big, strong walls. Before the invention of gunpowder, catapults were the best weapon to attack a city or castle. The arm holding the stones is held down, under tension, so it is trying to pull away from whatever is holding it in place. When the tension is released, the arm swings round and shoots out the stone. Catapults could shoot heavy stones and even rotting animal bodies!

Draw the curving path, or trajectory, of each missile being fired from these catapults. Choose different missiles and see if any of them will hit the castle under siege.

(Answers on page 30.)

SPIN CYCLE

Have you tried washing any clothes by hand? It's very hard work. Washing machines automatically fill up with water, add soap powder or liquid, heat up the water, jumble the clothes around so the dirt falls off, rinse them several times and then spin them to dry them as much as possible.

Machines wash a lot more clothes than you could do by hand. Can you match these pairs and find the odd socks?

(Answers on page 30.)

ZIPPING ALONG

Finish off this zipper. Then decorate the pencil case.

On either side of a zipper is a row of links. These links are exactly the same size and exactly the same space apart so you can count: link, space, link, space, link, space and so on. One side of the zipper starts with a link at the bottom and the other side starts with the space at the bottom so when you zipper up your coat the slider (the piece you hold) joins the links together.

Before zippers were invented at the beginning of the 1900s, clothes were fastened with buttons or hooks-and-eyes and it took a lot longer to dress. Rich people even had servants to help them get dressed! Now there are even airtight zippers for deep-sea divers or space suits. This is an example of how simple technology can really change people's lives.

Color in all the outfits that need zips. Check your artwork on page 30.

HUFF AND PUFF

When you pull out the handle of a pump, it draws in air. Then you push the handle in and the air is pressed down, or compressed, at the bottom of the tube or chamber.

The pressure of the air opens a small valve, like a little gate, and the air rushes out through a narrow tube at a high speed. This blows up the ball...or the balloon or the bike tire.

Pump piston

Valve

Pump cylinder

Unravel this mess of pump tubes to find out who is pumping up their balloon the quickest.

(Answer on page 31.)

Check your answers on page 31.

Spot 20 differences between these two scenes. The family on the bottom need a new pump!

BRIDGING THE DIVIDE

Truss Bridge

Arch Bridge

There are lots of different types of bridges. Can you get this family from their home to the beach, crossing every bridge only once?

(Answer on page 31.)

Beam Bridge

Cable-Stayed Bridge

Suspension Bridge

Cantilever Bridge

Tied-Arch Bridge

Bridges work using compression and tension. Compression is the force used when you push something together. Tension is the force used when you pull something apart. If you get the right amount of each of these things then you can create a very strong structure. Bridges use their own weight in different ways to stay up. It's a clever balancing act.

THE WORLD WIDE WEB

What do you think
the internet looks like?
Draw it here.

The internet is the way computers are connected to each other all over the world. They might be linked by wires or without wires, called wireless. You can use the internet to send email messages, chat online and make phone or video calls. You can also search for information on the web or world wide web (www). These are pages of information linked together by the internet. You find those pages through a web browser.

u	s	e	r	n	a	m	e	o	s	j	m	e	r	i	w
g	d	a	n	z	q	u	l	n	s	a	f	e	t	y	e
z	r	b	h	k	m	k	d	l	b	o	o	k	e	e	t
f	o	r	w	a	r	d	n	i	h	s	h	w	n	o	n
r	w	o	x	s	s	t	p	n	s	e	v	i	r	u	s
e	s	w	e	b	s	i	t	e	h	m	d	y	e	j	o
p	s	s	r	h	l	g	r	i	a	a	i	w	t	f	c
l	a	e	a	p	g	d	p	k	o	i	k	l	n	p	i
y	p	r	j	k	d	g	s	s	e	l	e	r	i	w	a
b	e	k	r	a	m	k	o	o	b	e	m	e	i	l	l

website	bookmark	online	social
browser	wireless	virus	share
address	email	forward	username
internet	safety	reply	password

SNAPPY CHALLENGE

Before the invention of digital cameras, if you wanted a portrait of yourself or your favorite pet, an artist had to paint it for you. Early cameras were very large and heavy and took ages to take the photo. Now digital cameras are small and light and you can take photos with a tiny camera in a mobile phone.

Draw a selfie!

When you point your camera at something, light travels from the scene or object you are photographing into the camera through a lens. This light then hits a sensor, which is divided into millions of little squares, called pixels. Each pixel represents a different color or brightness. The computer in the camera converts the pixels into a picture.

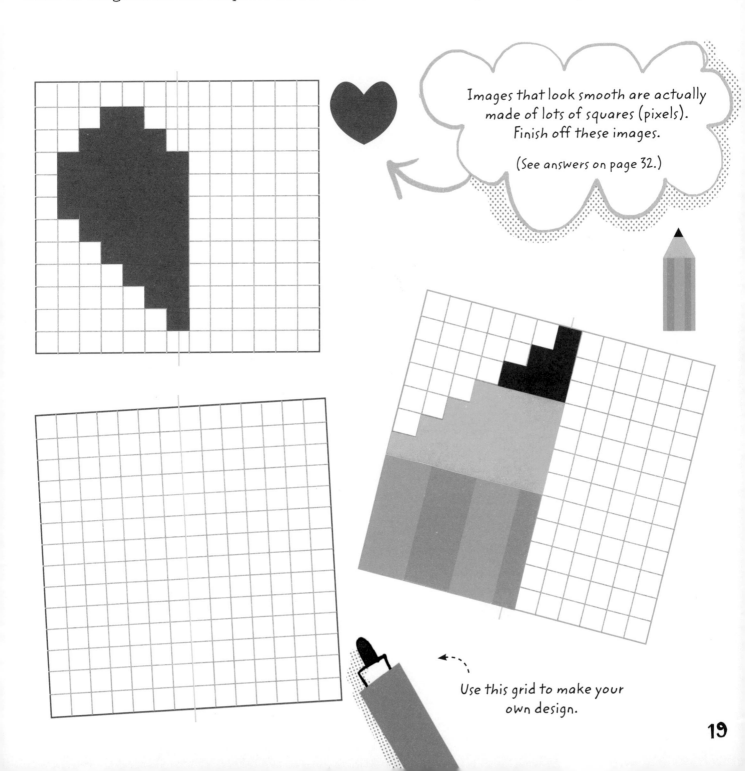

Images that look smooth are actually made of lots of squares (pixels). Finish off these images.

(See answers on page 32.)

Use this grid to make your own design.

TALKING ON THE TELEPHONE

Before telephones were invented, if you wanted to talk to someone, you had to go to their house or meet them somewhere face to face. Now you can talk to friends on the other side of the world just by picking up the phone.

When you speak into a mobile phone, it sends a microwave to a special antenna and this antenna transmits (sends) it on to the telephone exchange. The exchange turns it into a digital message to send on to the person you are speaking to, along a cable or sometimes by satellite. Your mobile phone won't work properly if there isn't an antenna nearby so there are mobile phone antennas everywhere. Look for them when you go out.

SHAKE IT UP

Read below about how these microwaves heat up your food. See how quickly you can follow the waves with your pencil. Make sure you stay in the lines! Time yourself and write your best score below.

Microwaves are a type of radio wave. The wave wobbles the molecules in the liquid part of your food and, as the molecules jumble about and crash together, they heat up. Microwaves only travel in one direction. So that's why the food goes round and round on the tray in the oven, to make sure the microwaves pass through all parts of the food and cook it thoroughly.

WHEELY USEFUL

Can you spot these things in this busy basketball scene? (Answers on page 32.)

2 x basketballs   4 x water bottles
6 x headbands   1 x butterfly
3 x birds   1 x baseball cap
2 x blue socks   1 x flag

A wheelchair means that people who have difficulty walking can go to work, visit friends, go shopping and play sports. Wheelchairs can be electric and are powered by batteries. Some wheelchairs have large rubber wheels so they can go on snow or into water. Sports wheelchairs need to be much lighter than standard wheelchairs so the athlete can whiz around the court.

GPS KNOWS THE WAY

Think of the route from your house to your school. Can you draw the map?

Explorers in ancient times sailed across the oceans using the sun, moon and stars to find their way. They didn't have accurate maps. In fact they drew the coastline of the countries they discovered and created the maps for the voyagers who followed them. Now maps are digital (the information is stored in a computer) and you can check your position on a phone or on a small computer in a car. This is especially useful for ships and aeroplanes. GPS (Global Positioning System) calculates your position from signals sent from satellites in space. The signal must come from at least four satellites to be accurate.

CHOCKS AWAY!

Air force pilots sometimes have to get out of their aircraft quickly to save their lives. They use an ejection seat. First, the pilot pulls a handle and the roof of the plane explodes off. A catapult then pushes the seat along some rails and out of the plane. Then a small rocket fires it away from the plane. Next a small parachute opens to slow the seat down. Finally the small parachute pulls the main parachute out and the seat is shot away so the pilot can float to earth safely.

This pilot has engaged his ejection seat! But these pictures are in the wrong order. Number them correctly.

(Answers on page 32.)

OPEN AND SHUT

All these things have hinges so you can open and shut them easily. What can you find in your house that has a hinge?

Make a list below.
And watch your fingers!

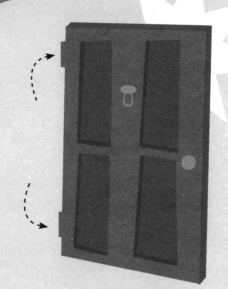

A hinge connects two solid pieces so that they can rotate, or turn, away from each other smoothly. Look for other hinges around the house. We have types of hinges in our body too. Can you think where?

Answer: fingers, toes, shoulders, knees and ankles   **27**

ON THE ROAD

Unlike gas-powered cars, electric cars don't pollute the air but they do need electricity to charge their batteries. They are much quieter than gas-powered cars and much cheaper to run. They can't do long journeys without being charged but most people only do short journeys in their cars anyway. Cars that don't need drivers are coming soon! Can you imagine what they will look like?

Draw a fantasy car. It's an electric car so you have to attach it to the electricity to power it up.

ANSWERS

Pages 6-7

Page 5

1. b) 19th November
2. b) three years
3. c) sheep's wool
4. They all do!
5. a) artificial trees

Pages 8-9

Page 11

Page 12

Page 13

Pages 14-15

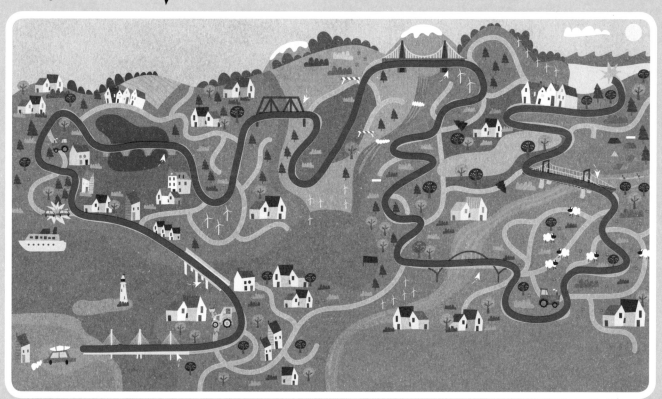

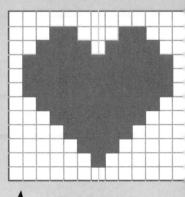

Page 19

Page 17

Page 23

Page 26

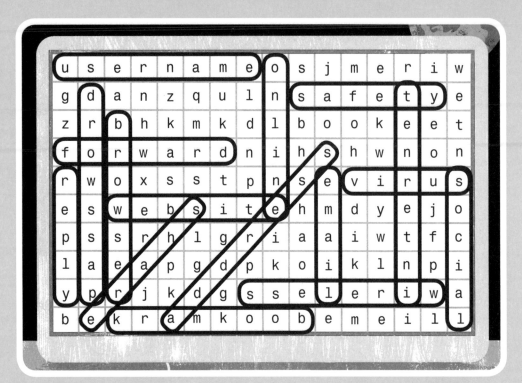